To the bright and imaginative minds that bring these pages to life with their colorful creativity. May your days be filled with joy, laughter, and endless adventures in the magical world of colors. Happy coloring!

Feel free to customize it to fit the theme or tone of your coloring book.

Priscilla Martins

2023

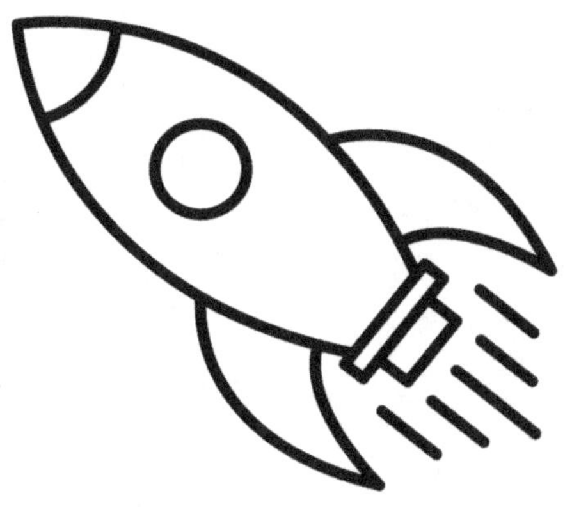
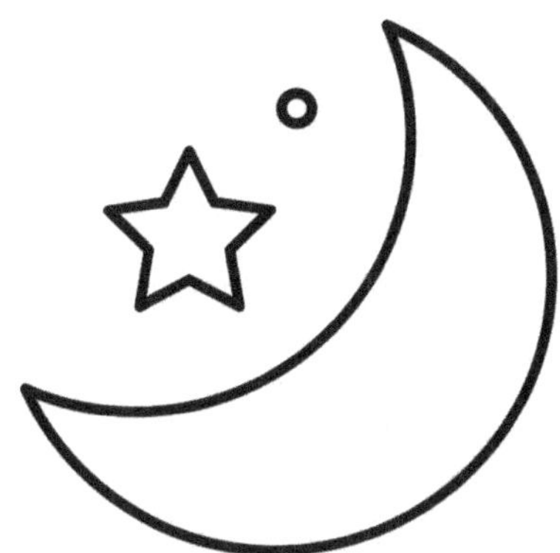

THIS BOOK BELONGS TO:

____

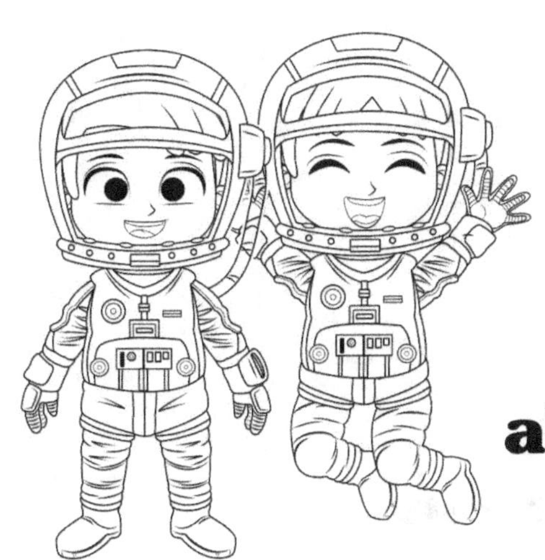

P.R.P.

all nights reserved

TEST COLOR PAGE

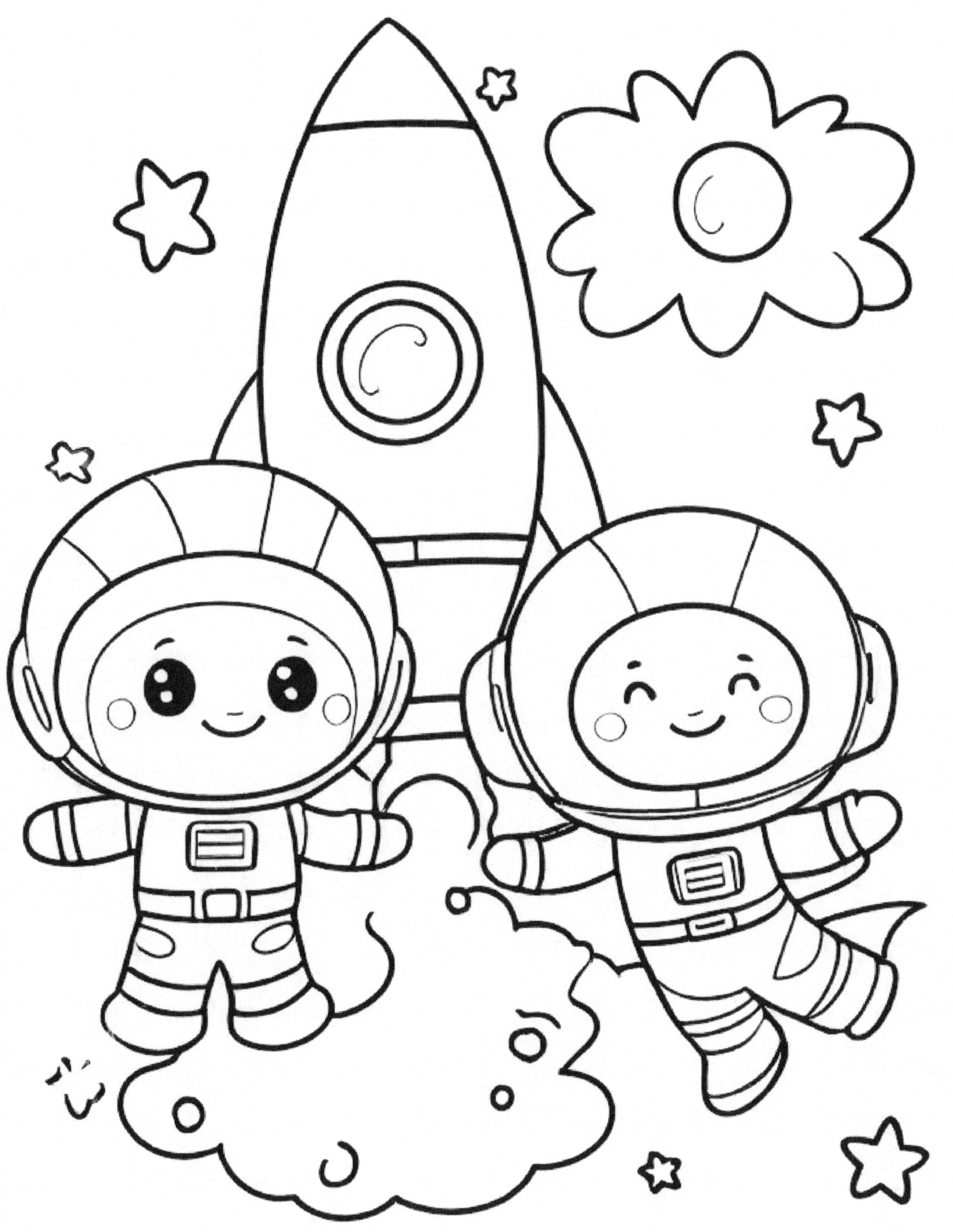

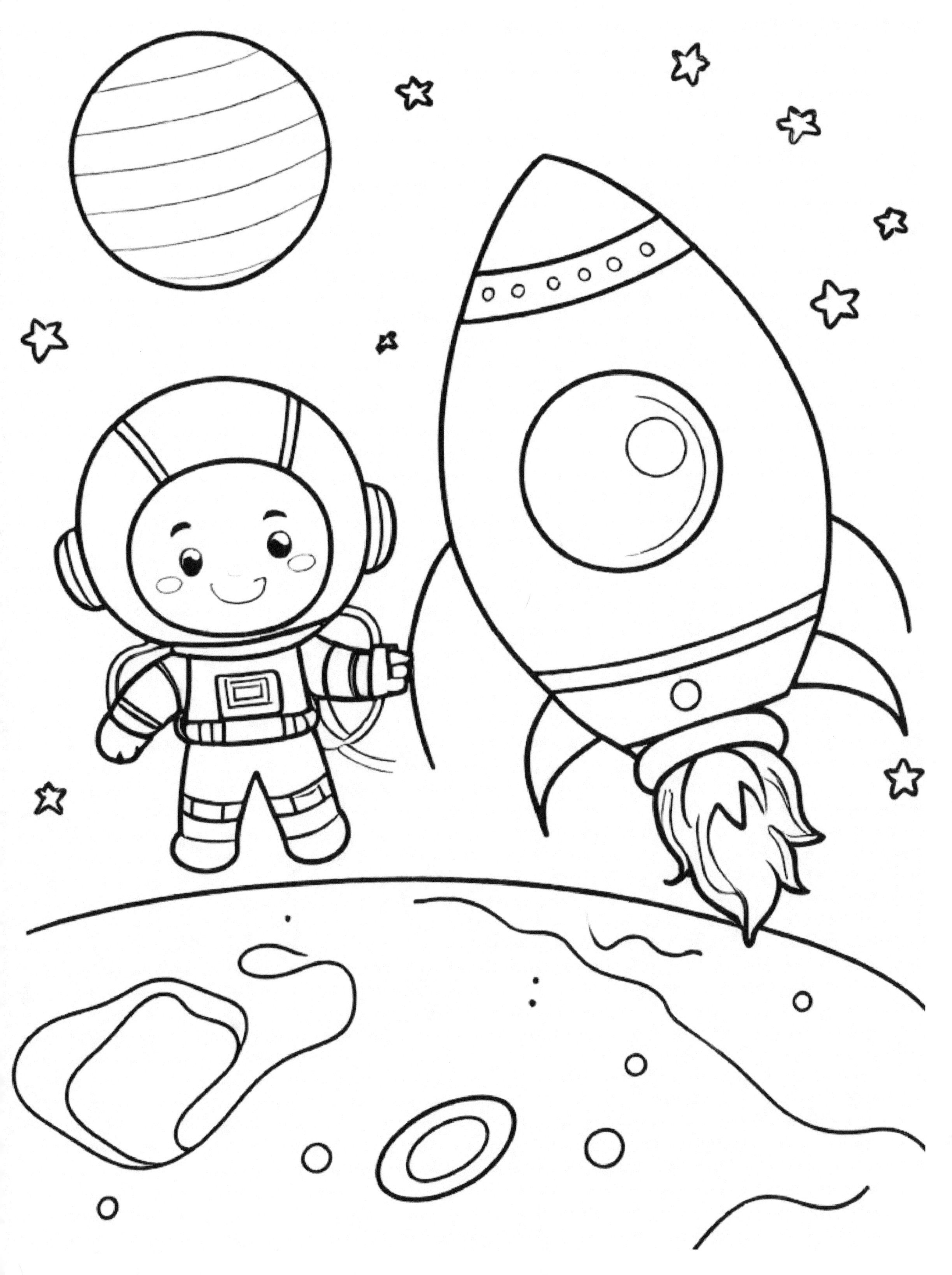

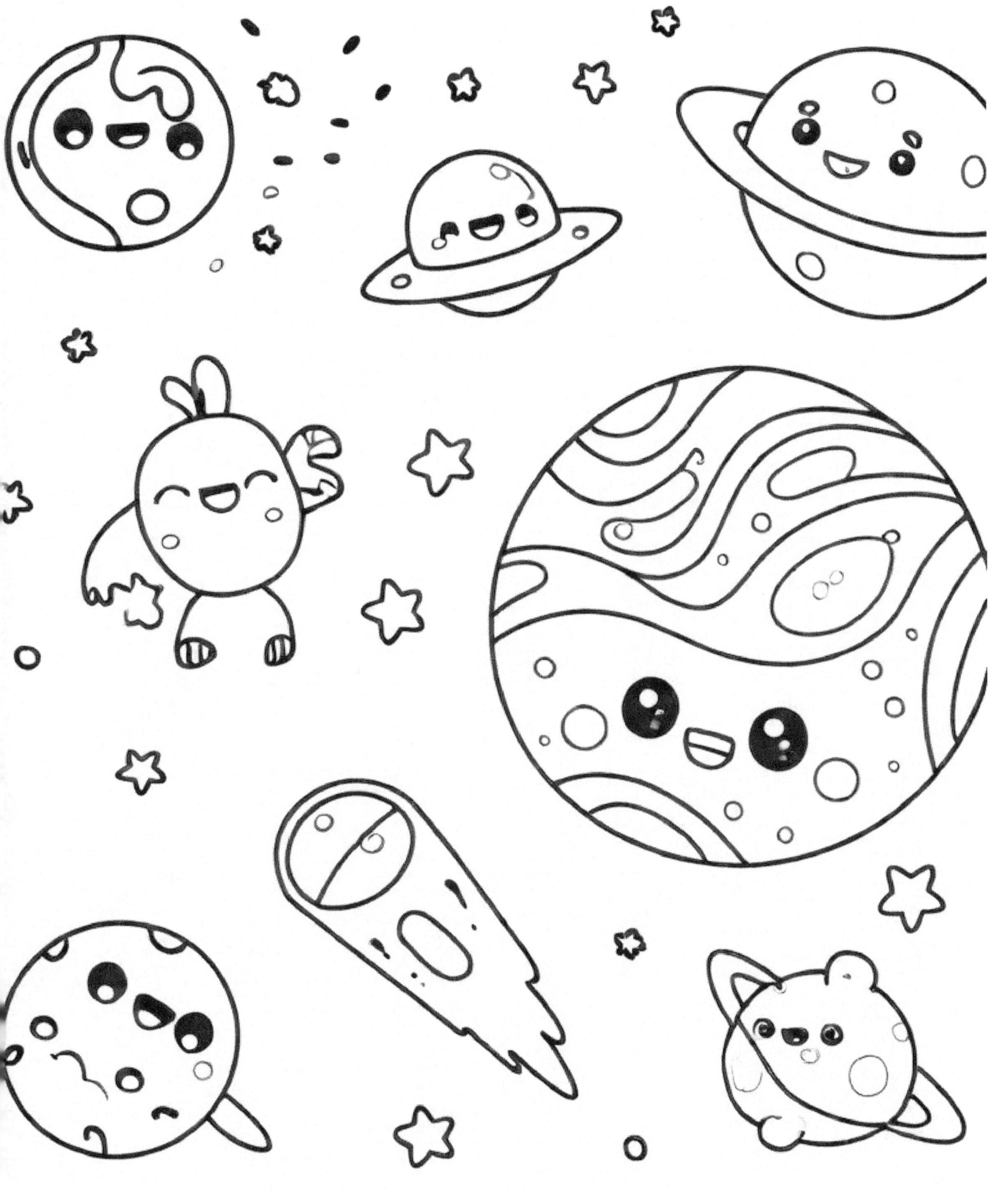

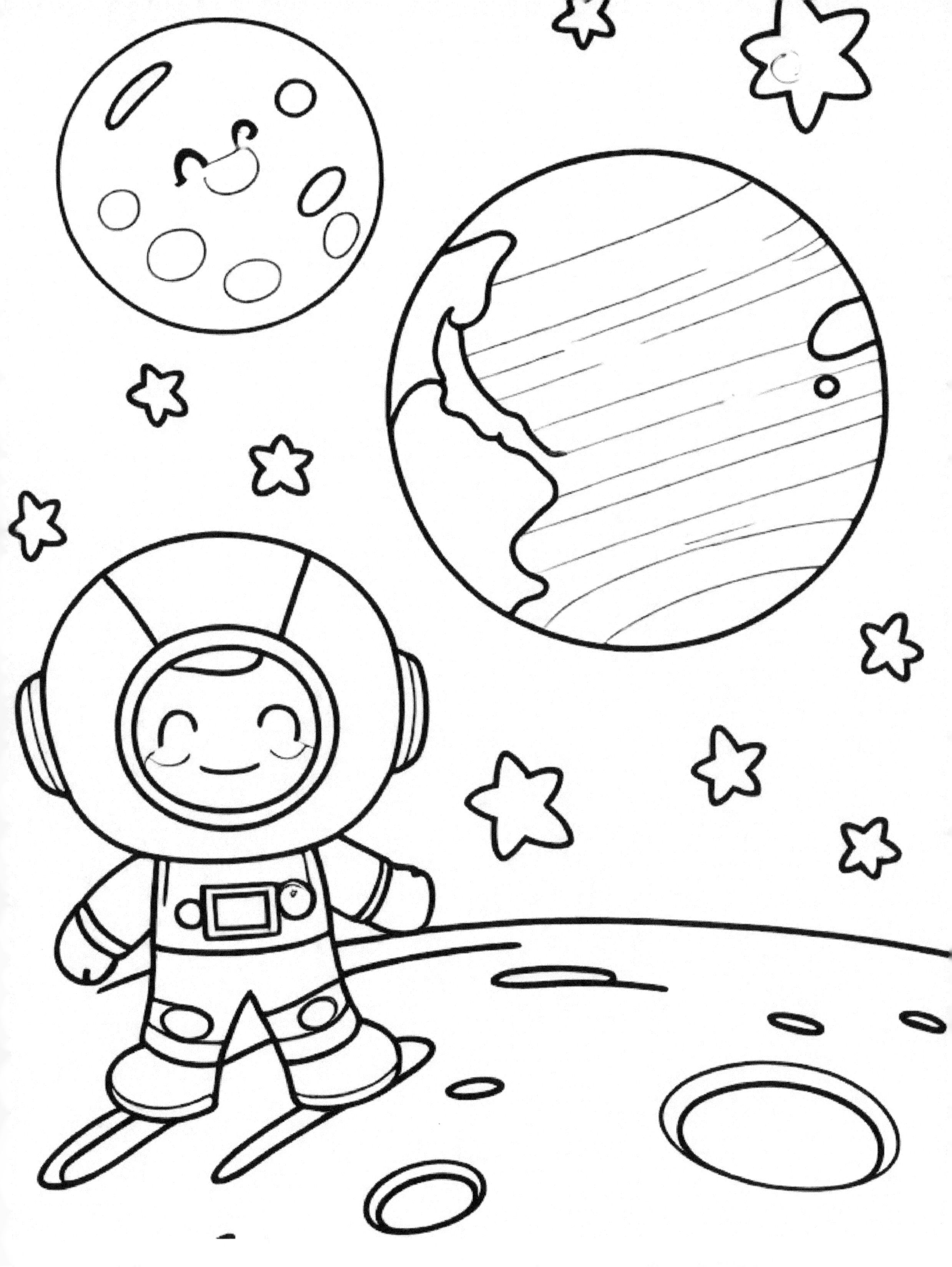

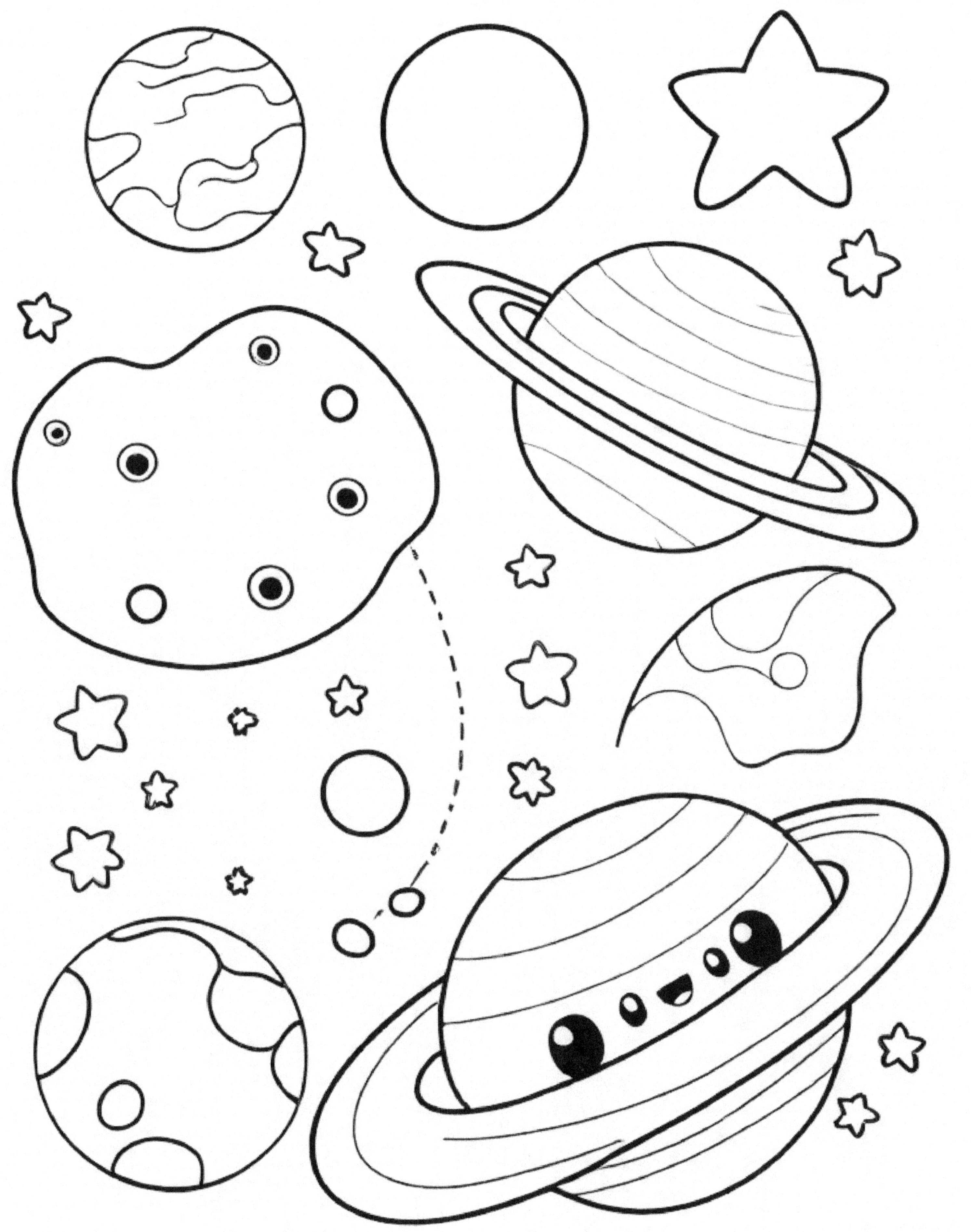

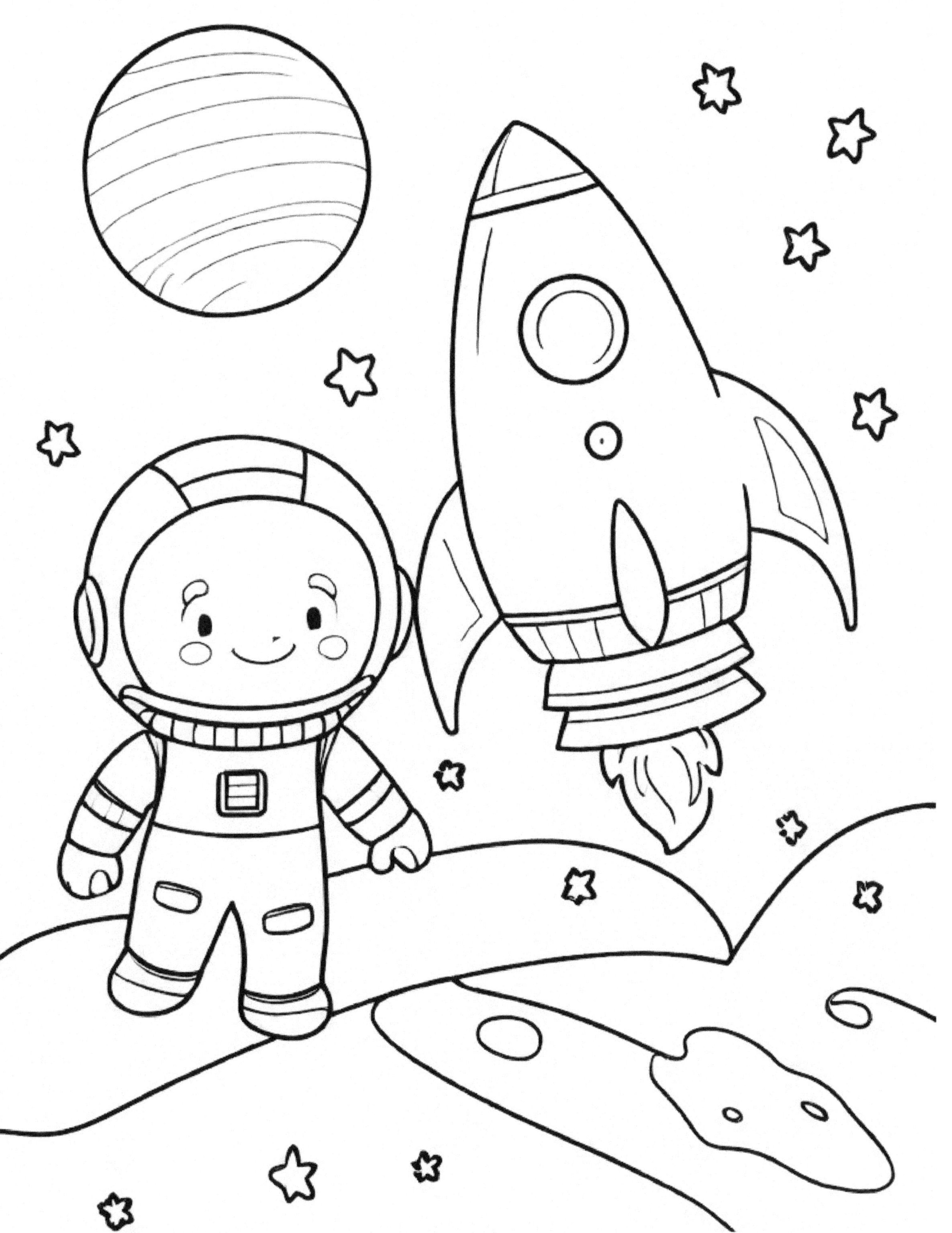

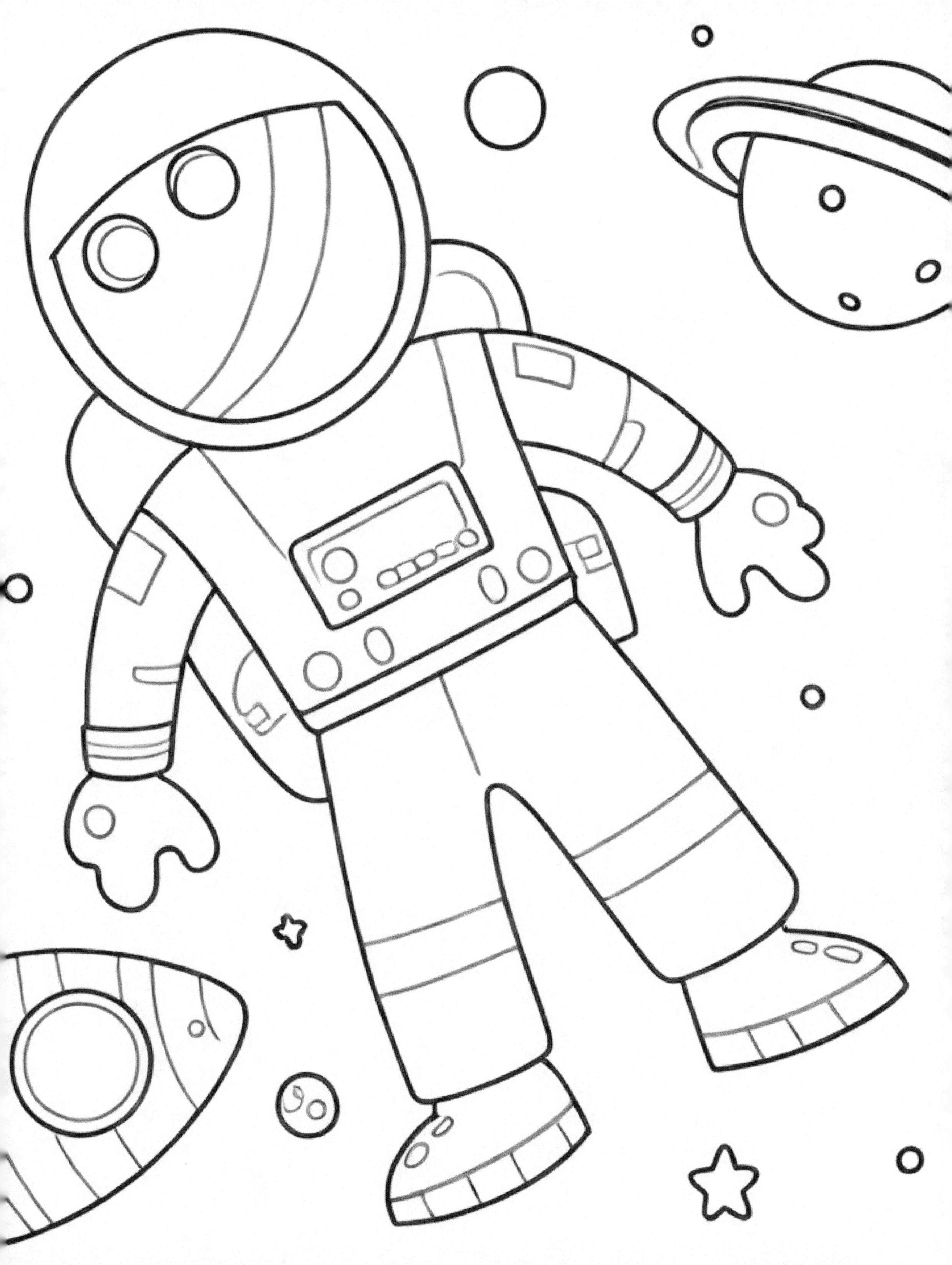

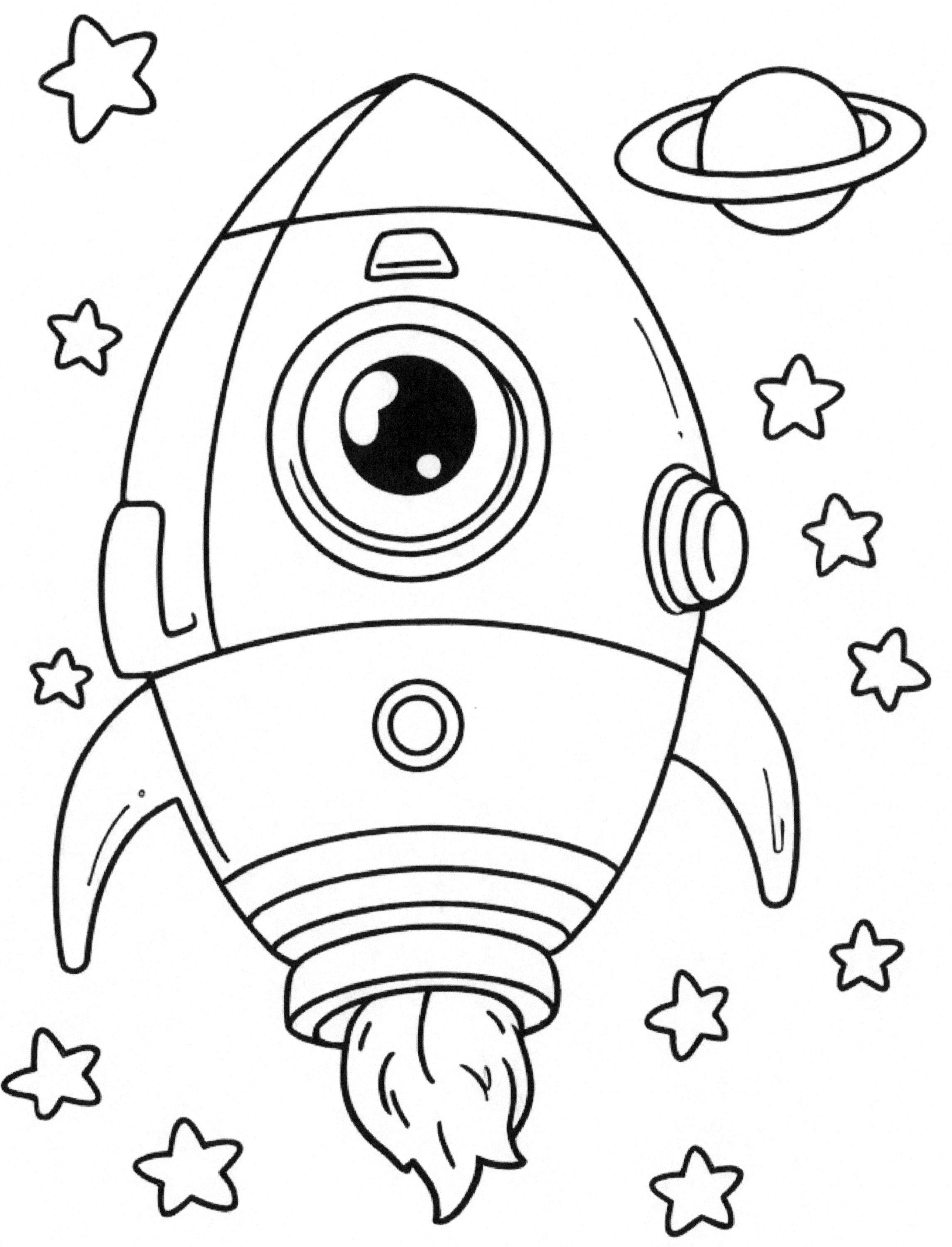

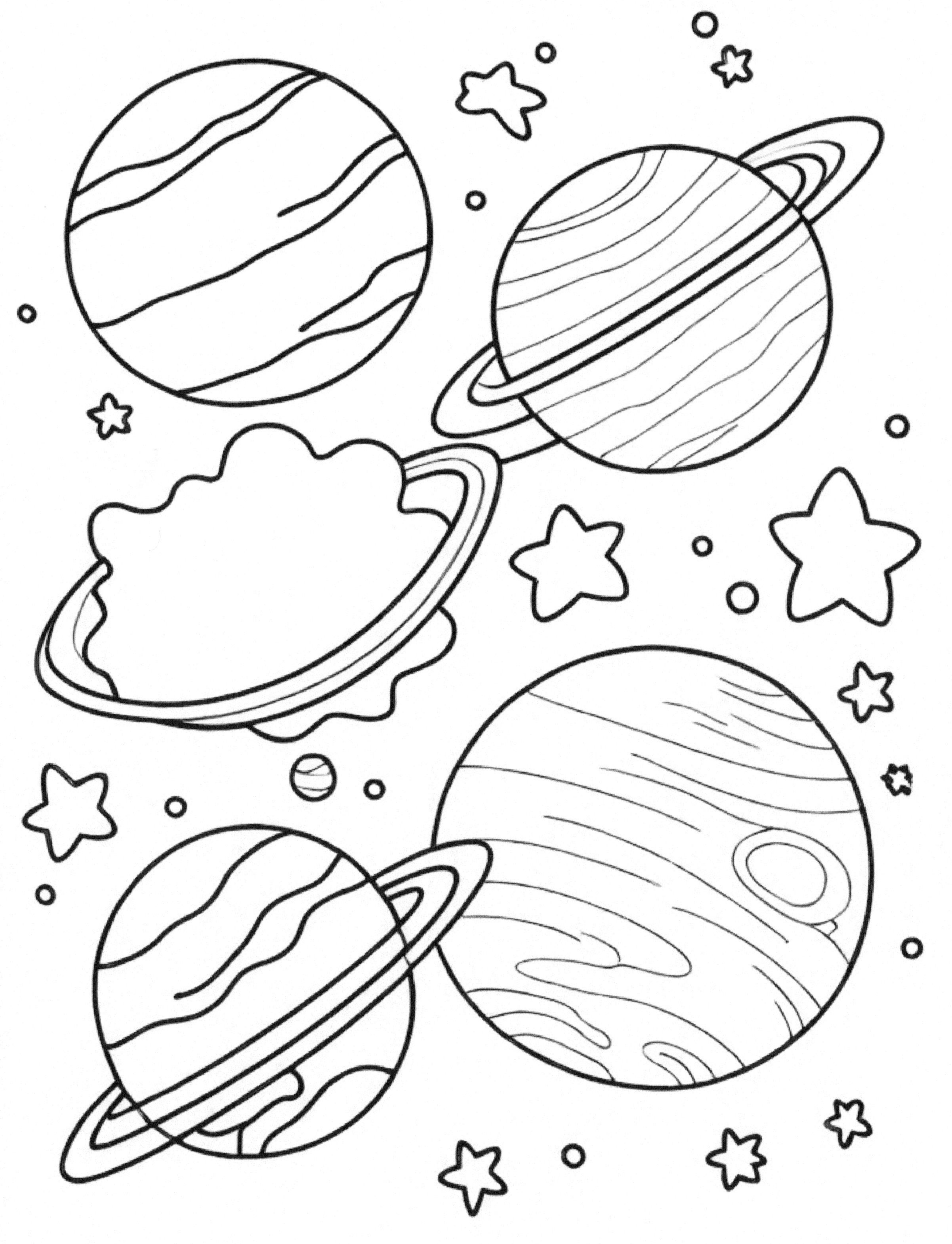

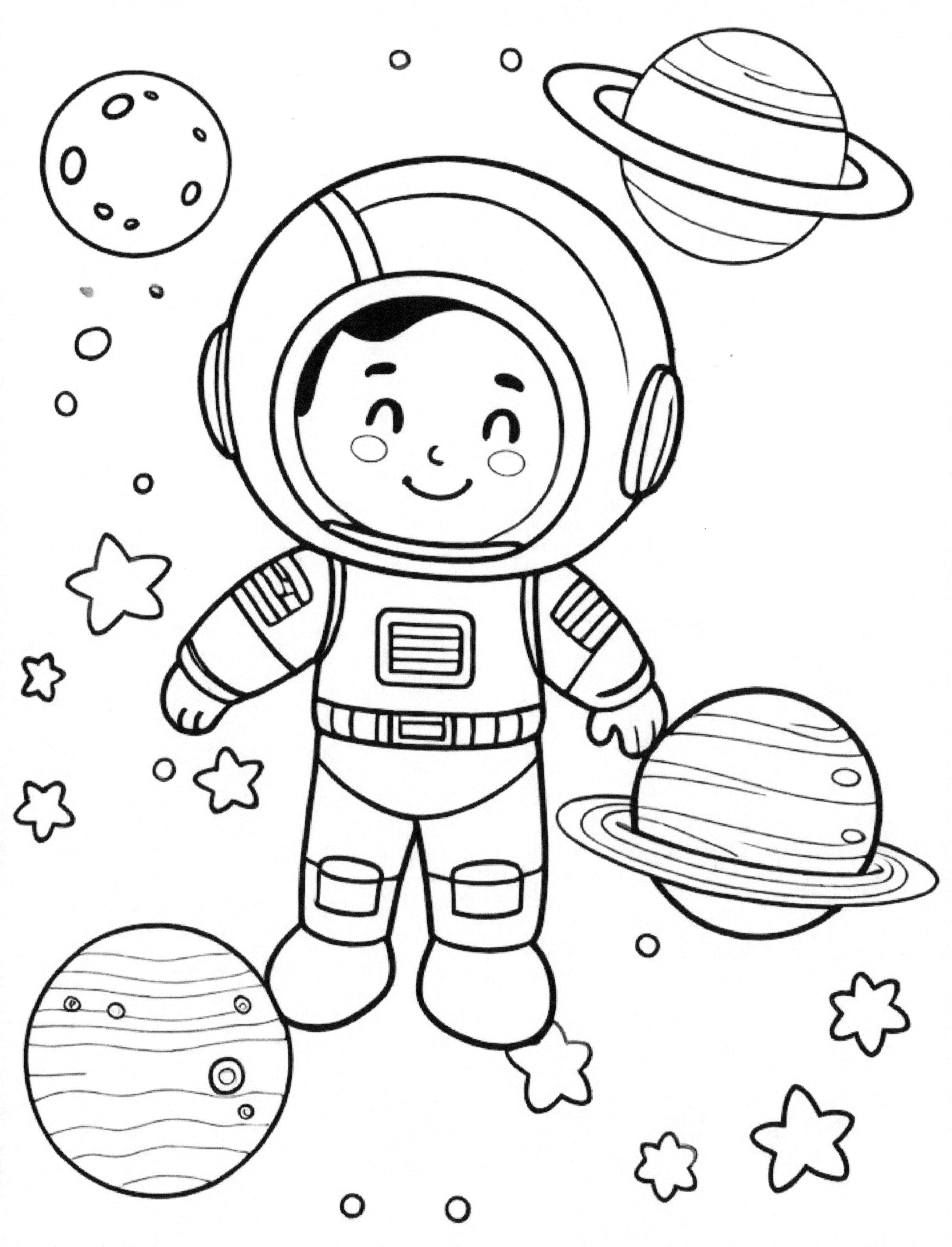

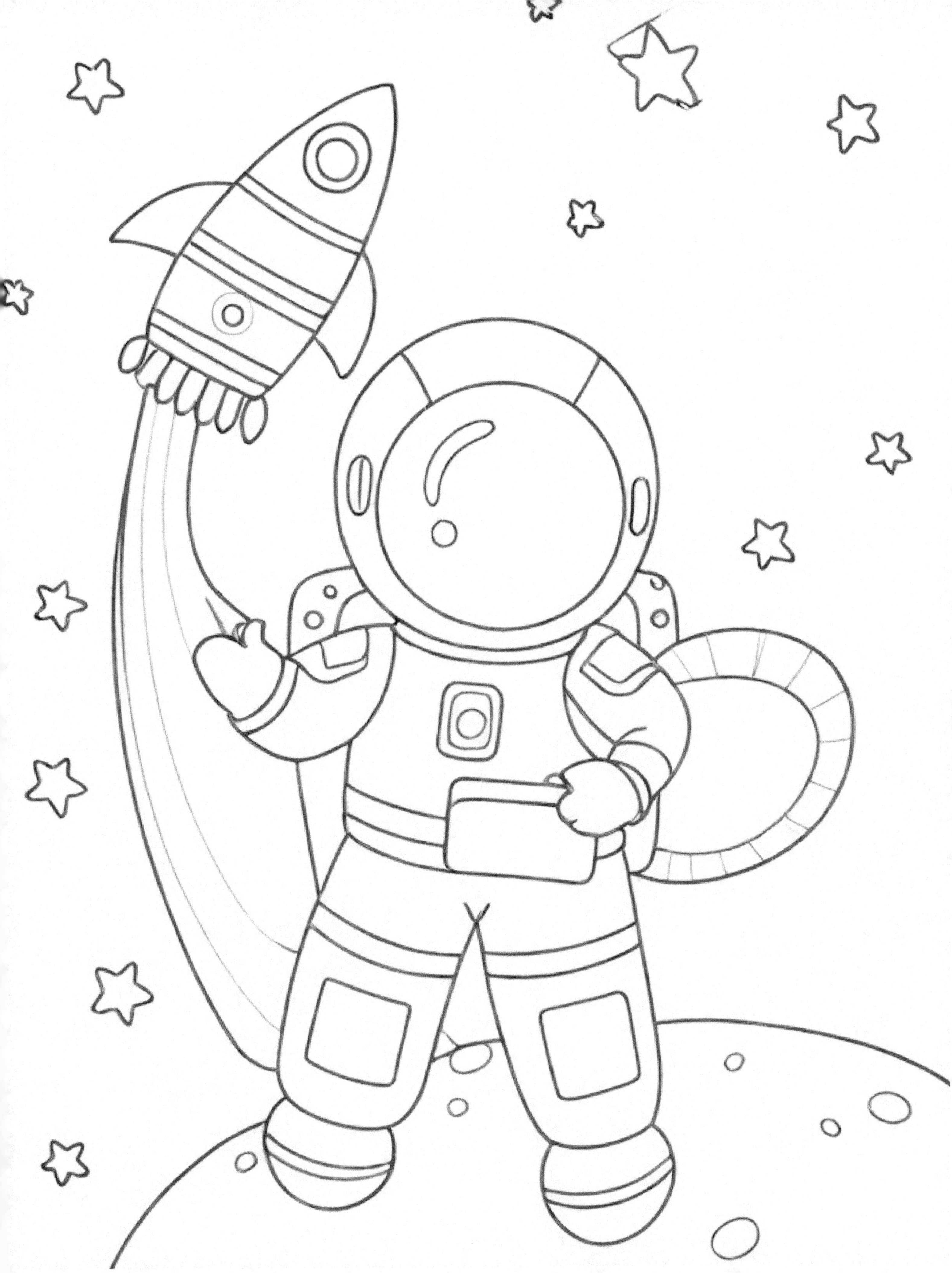

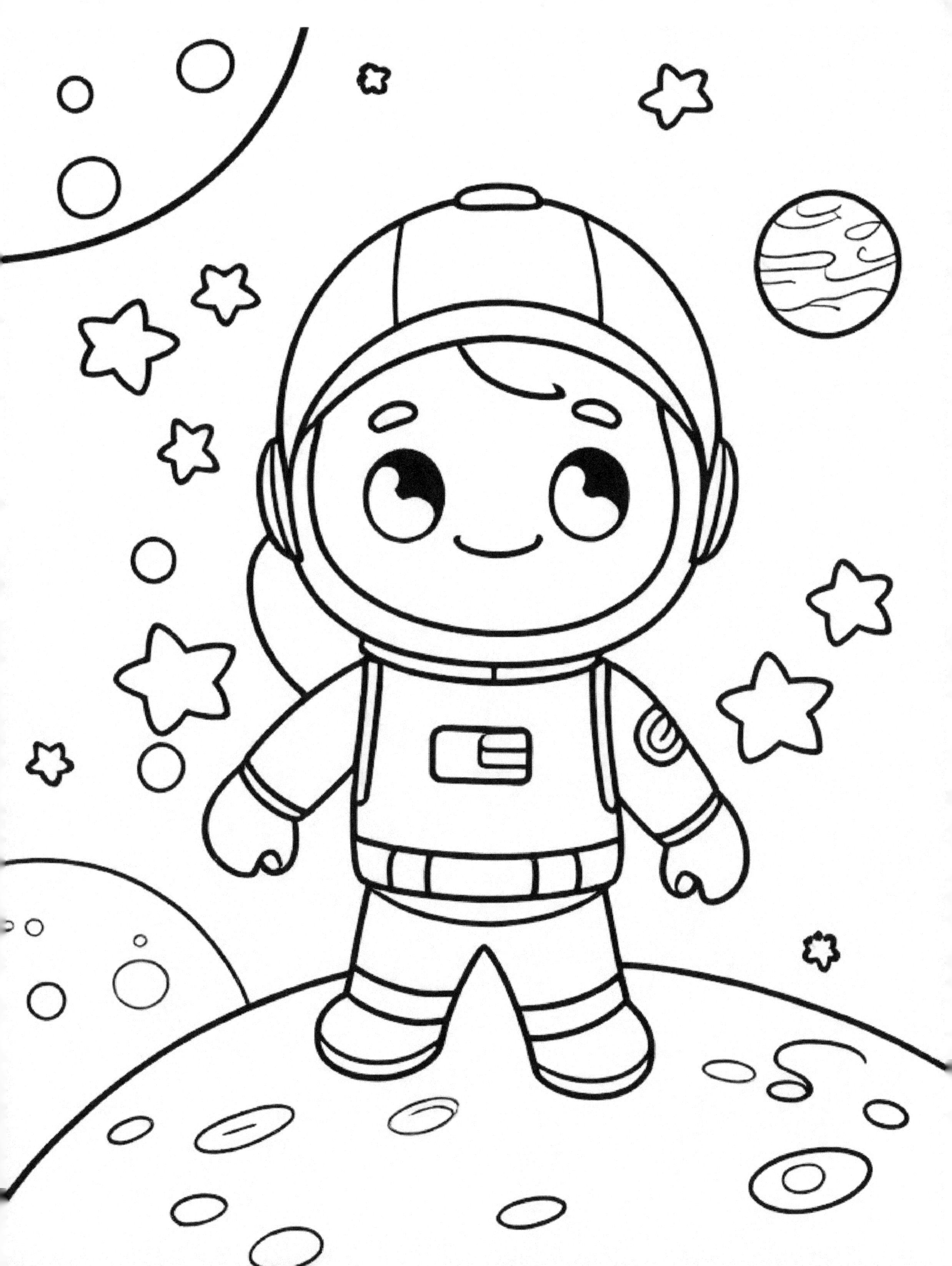

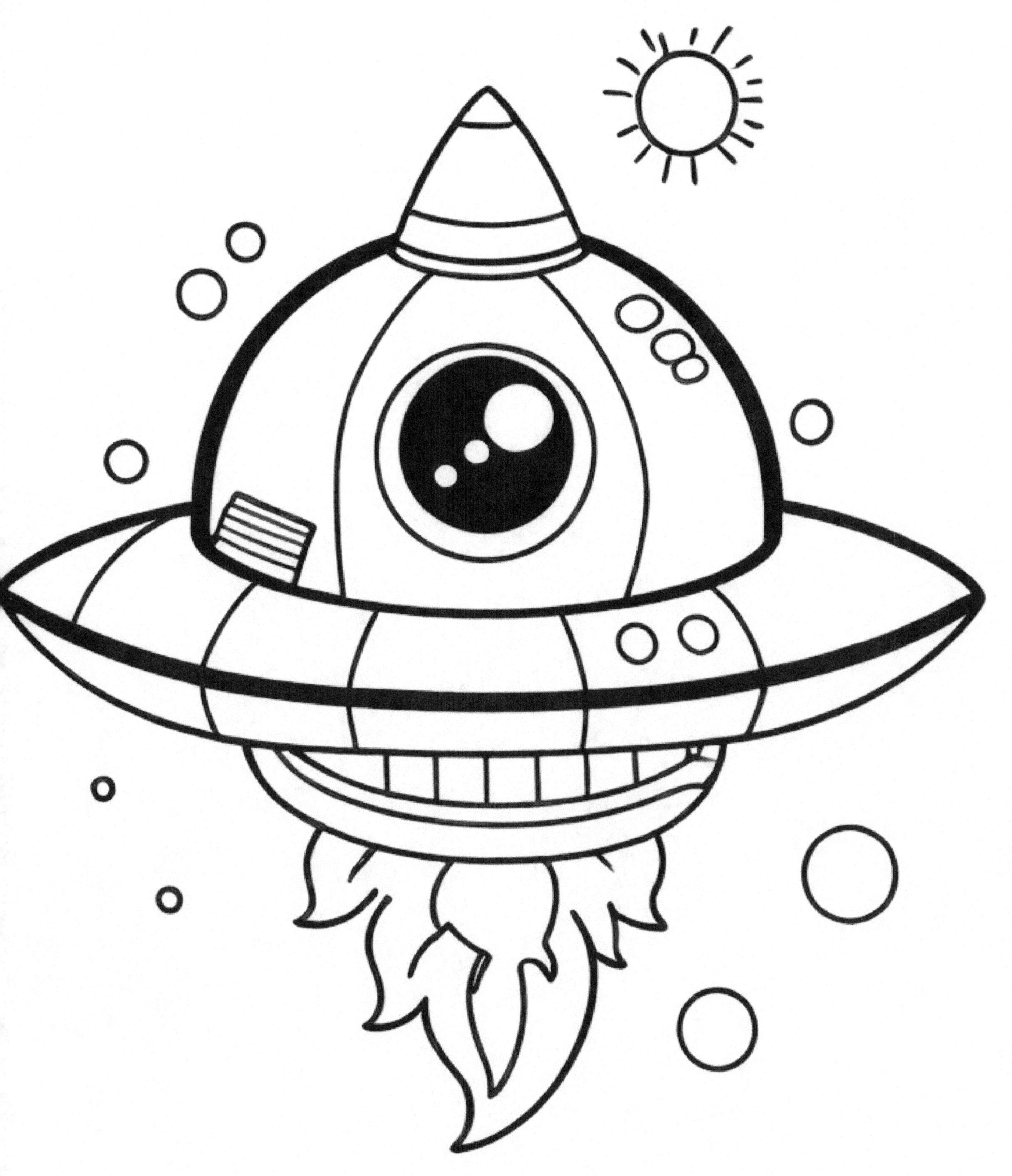

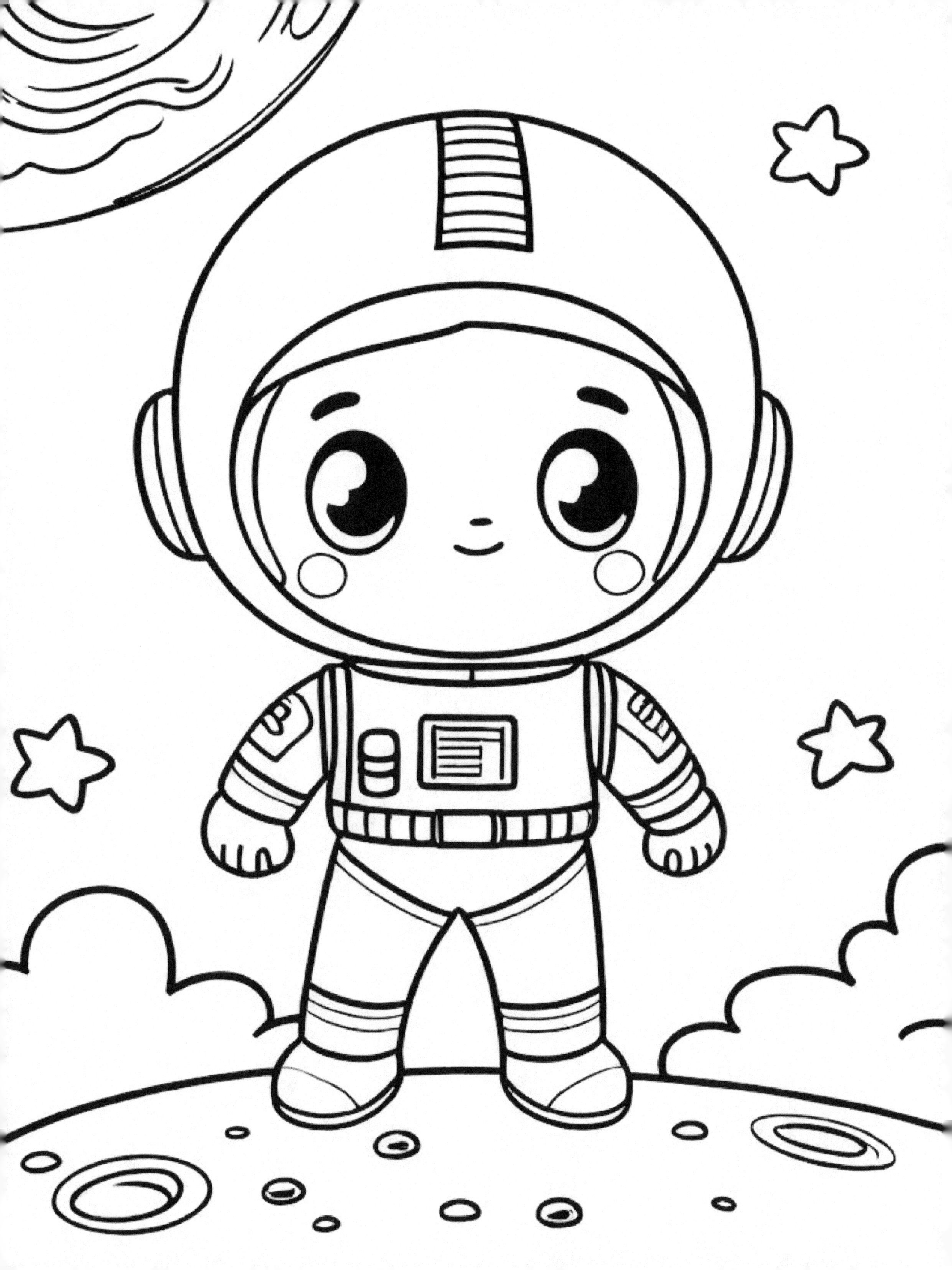

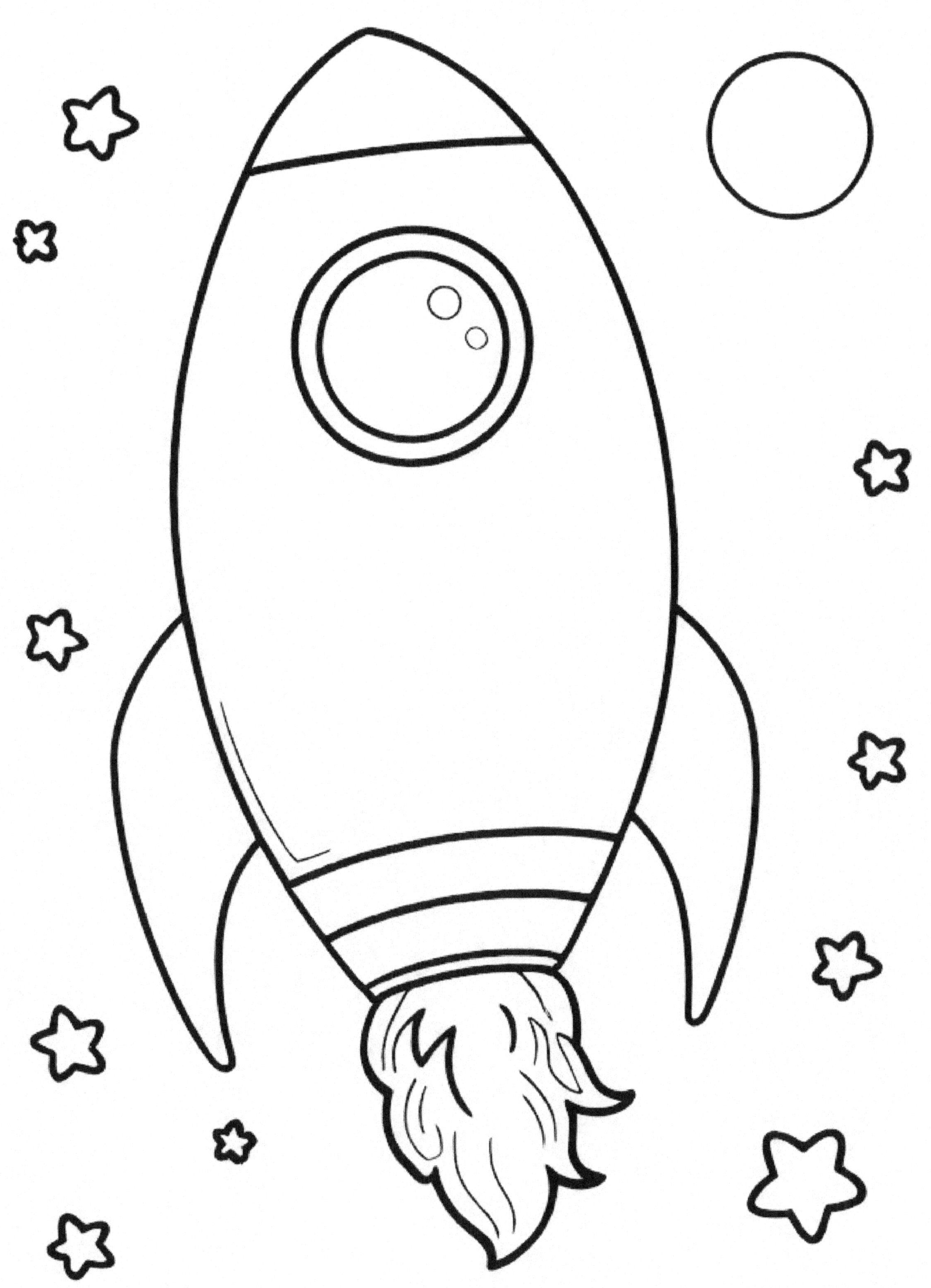

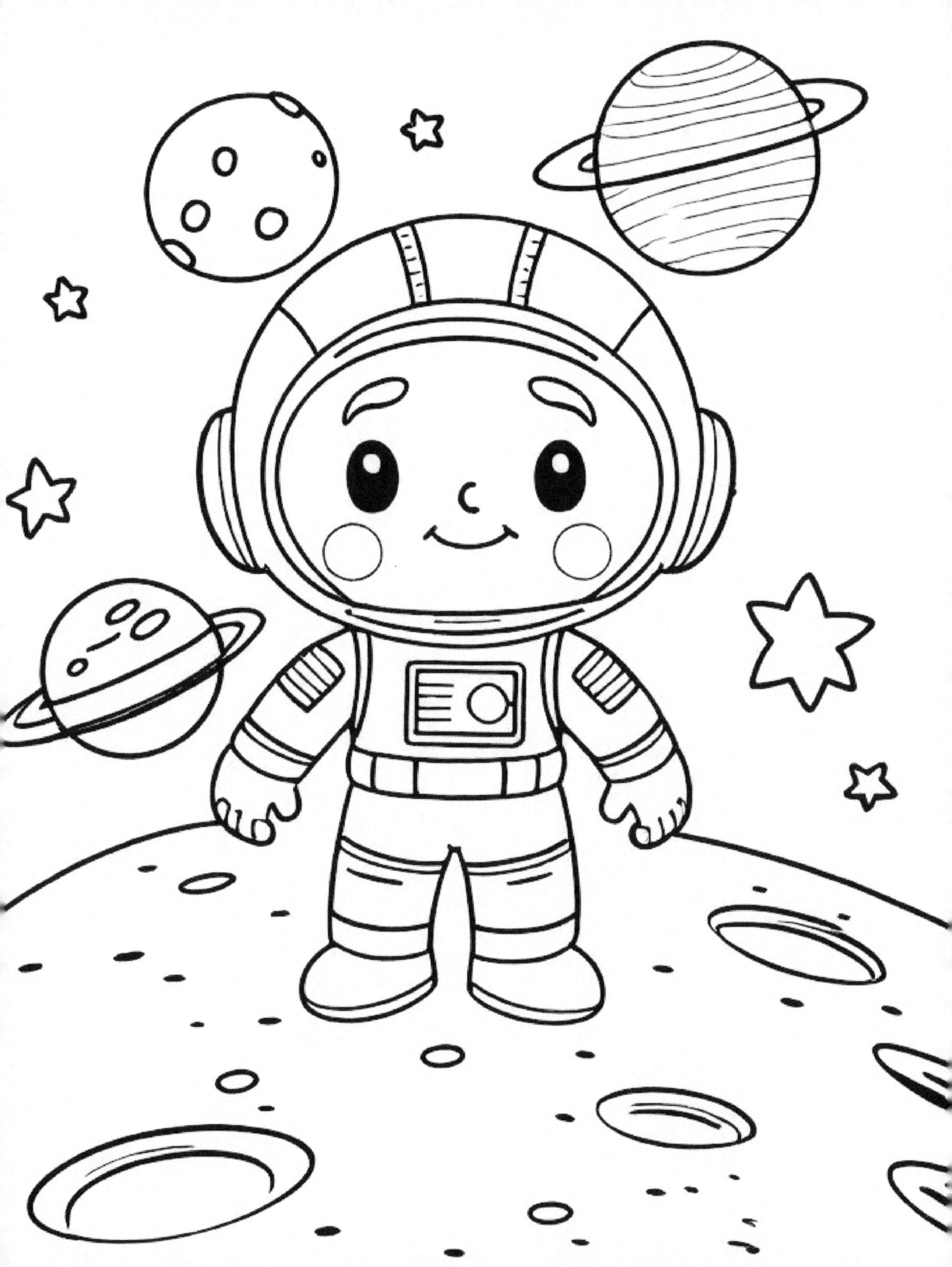

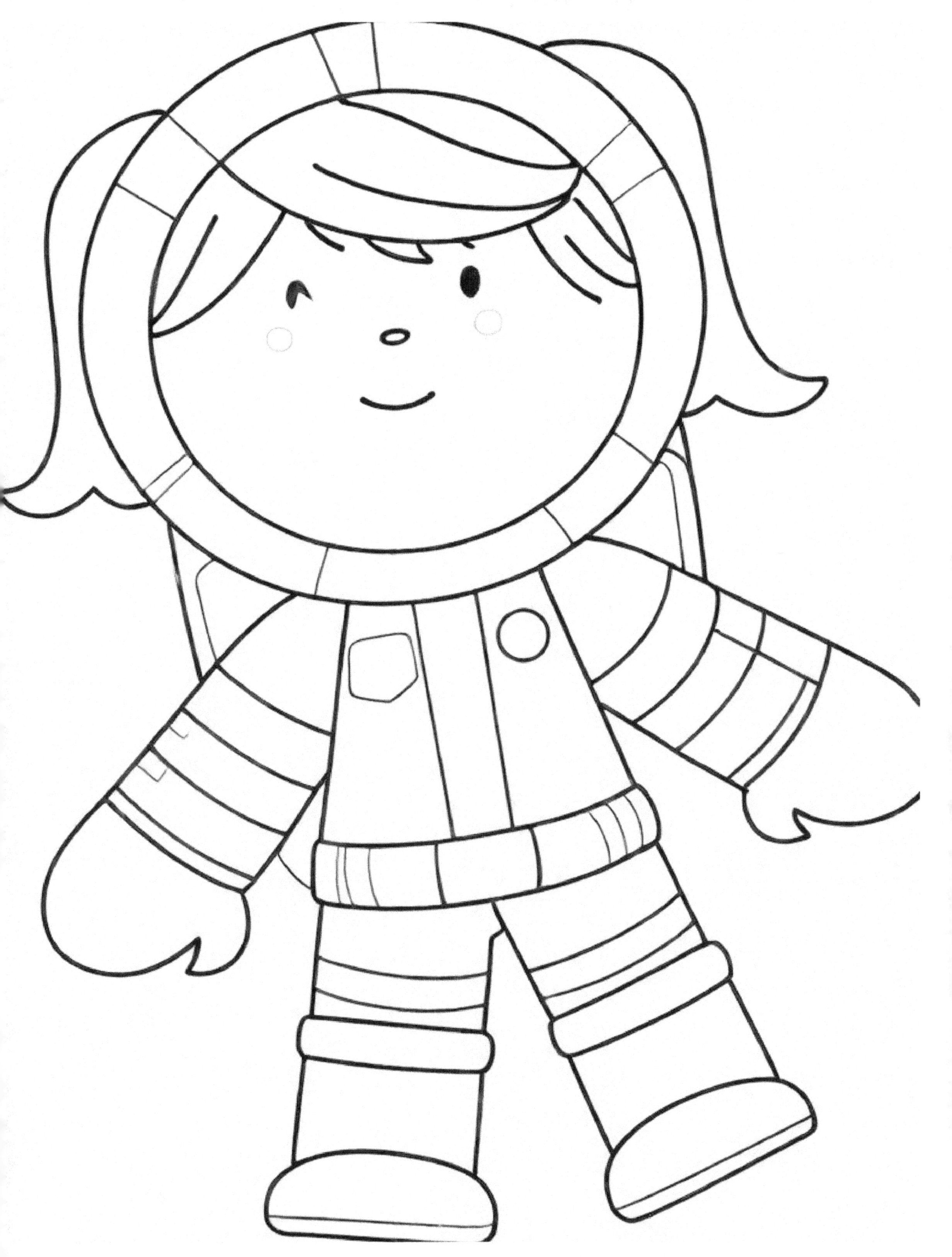

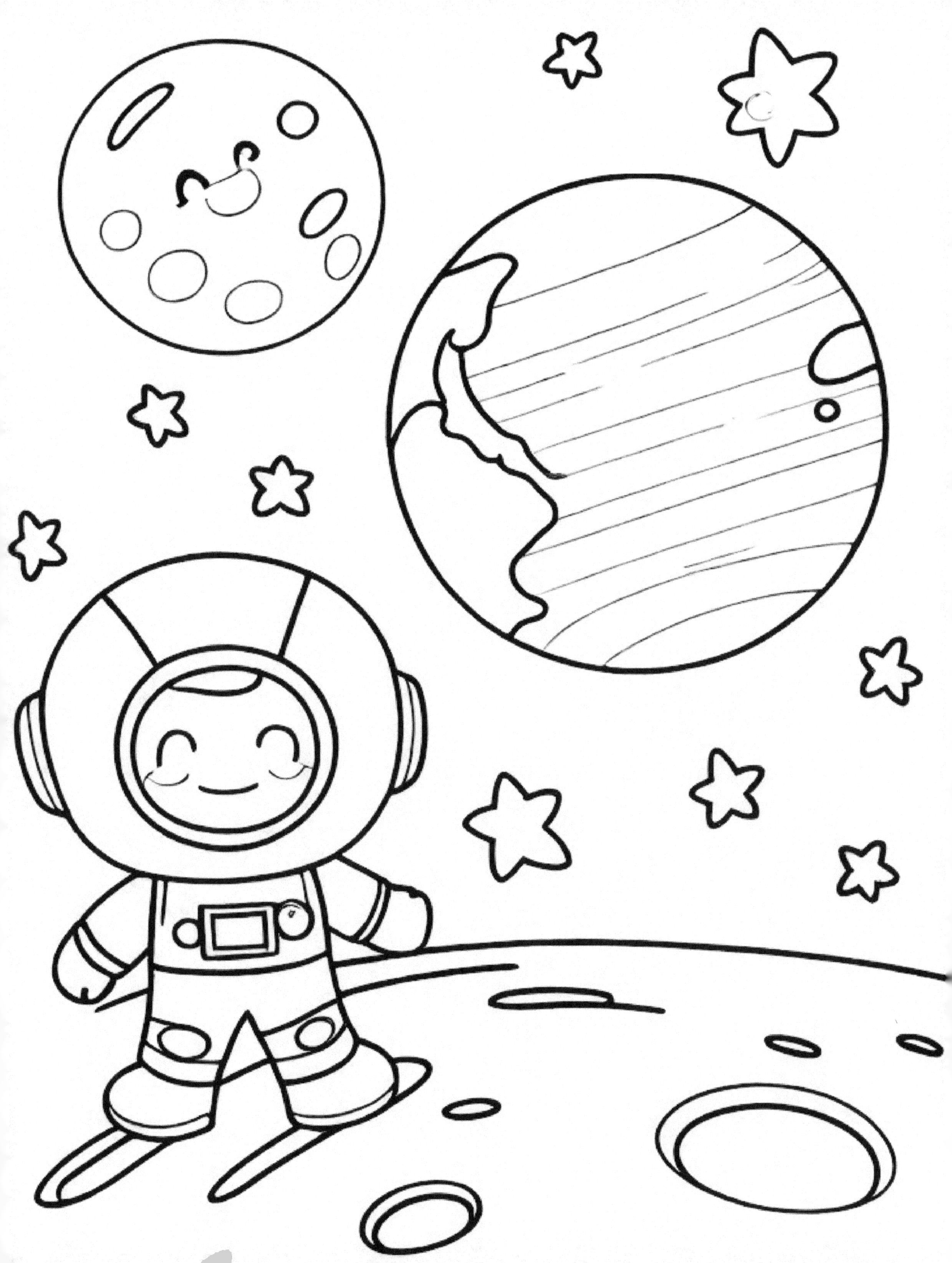

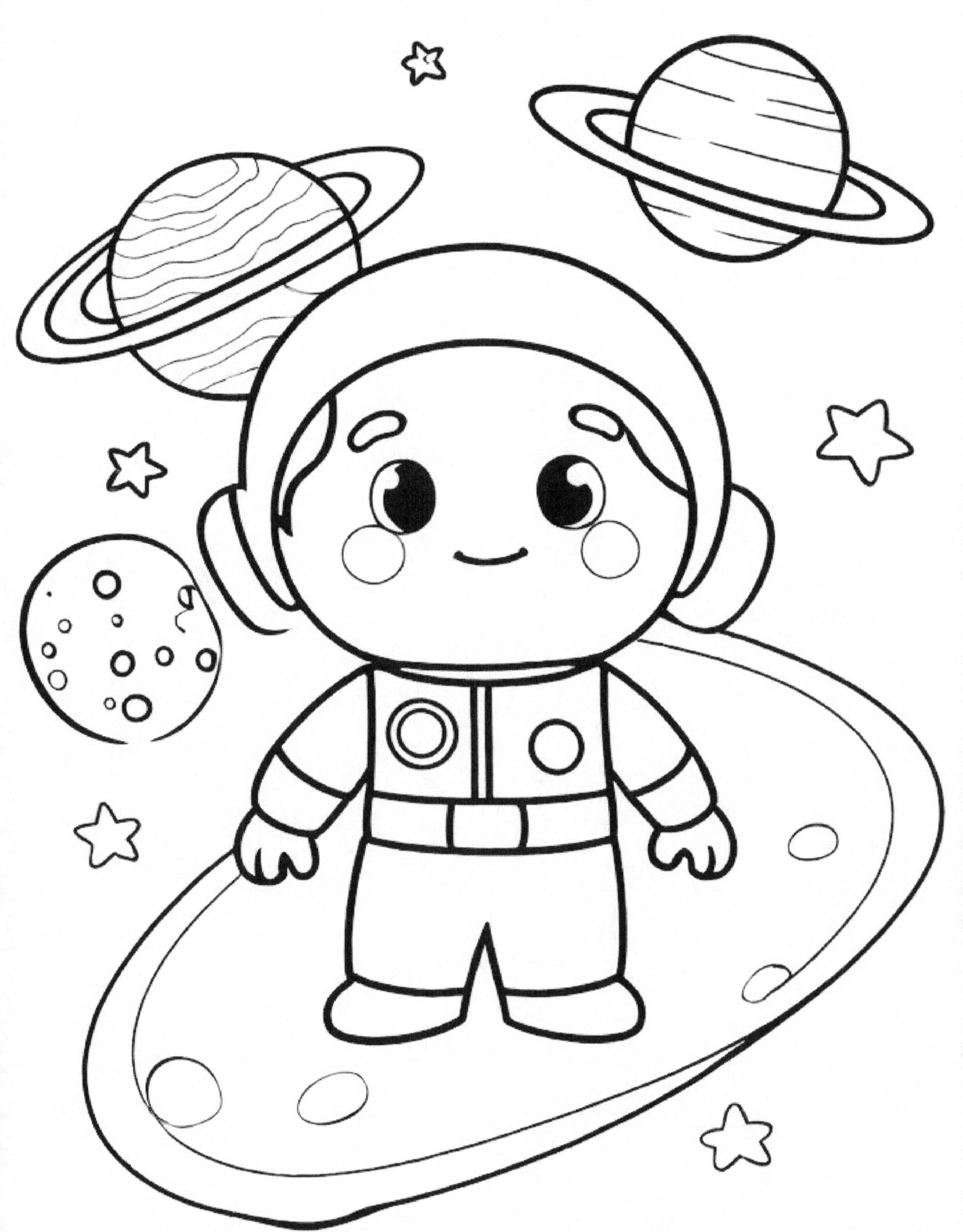

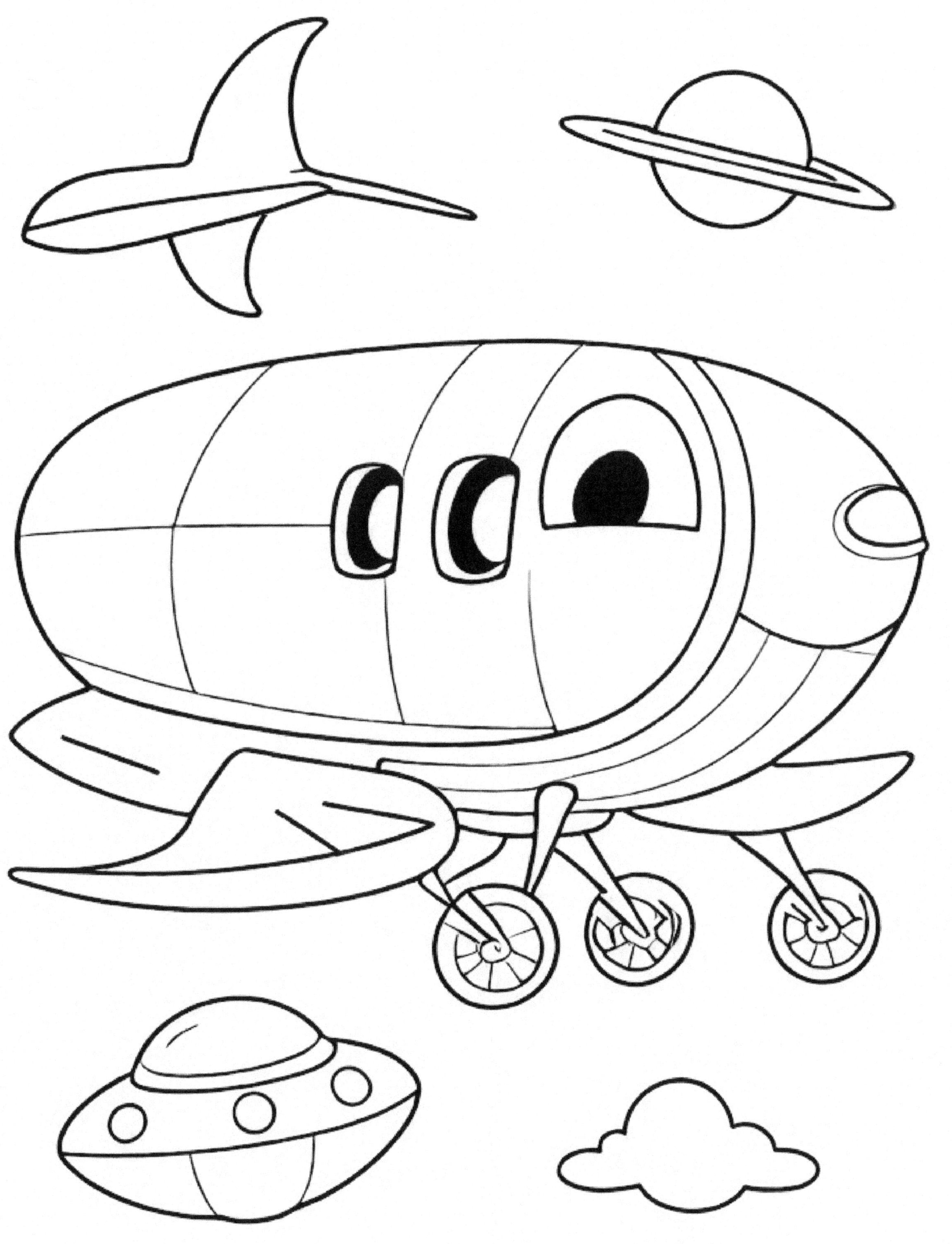

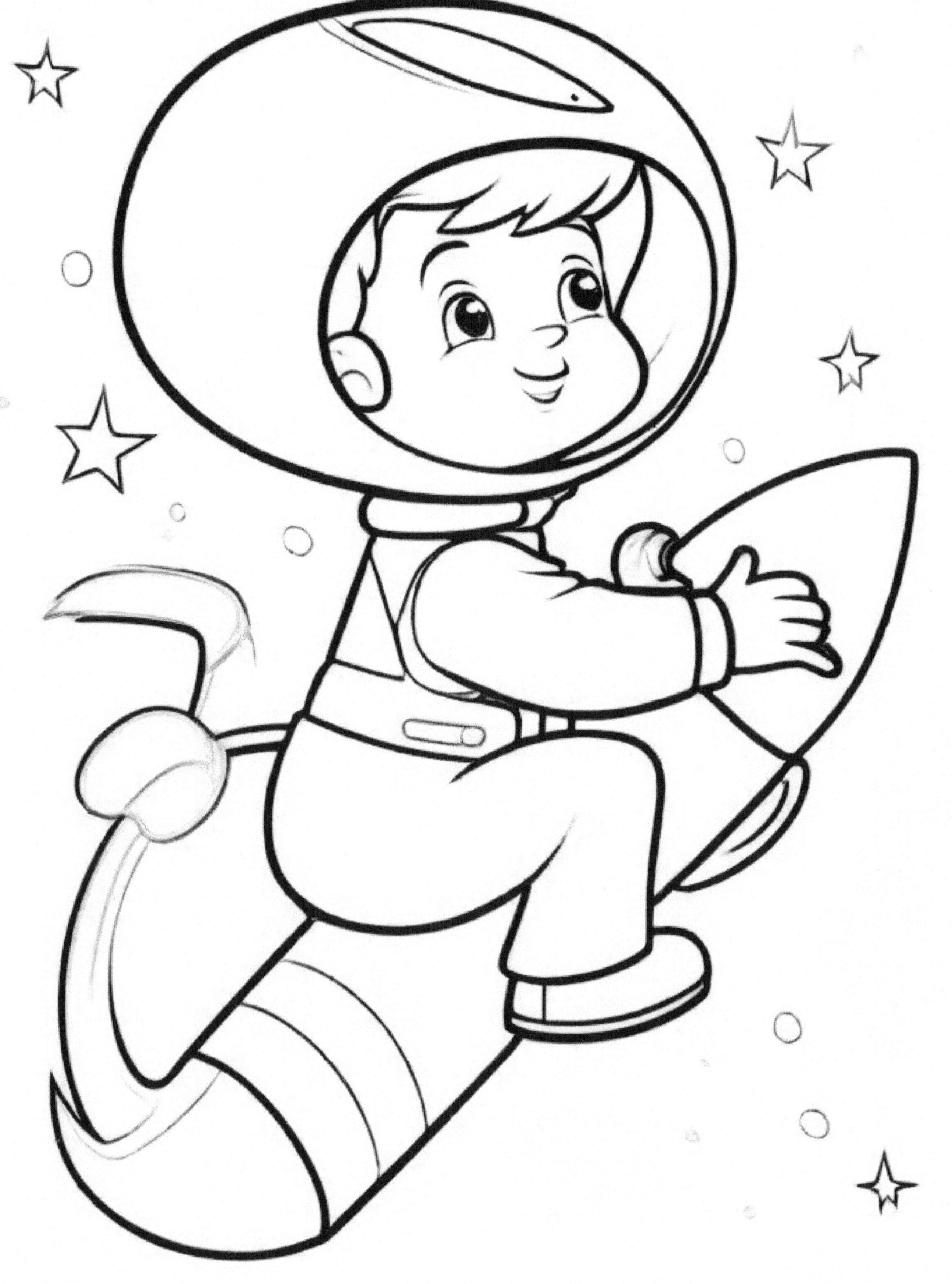

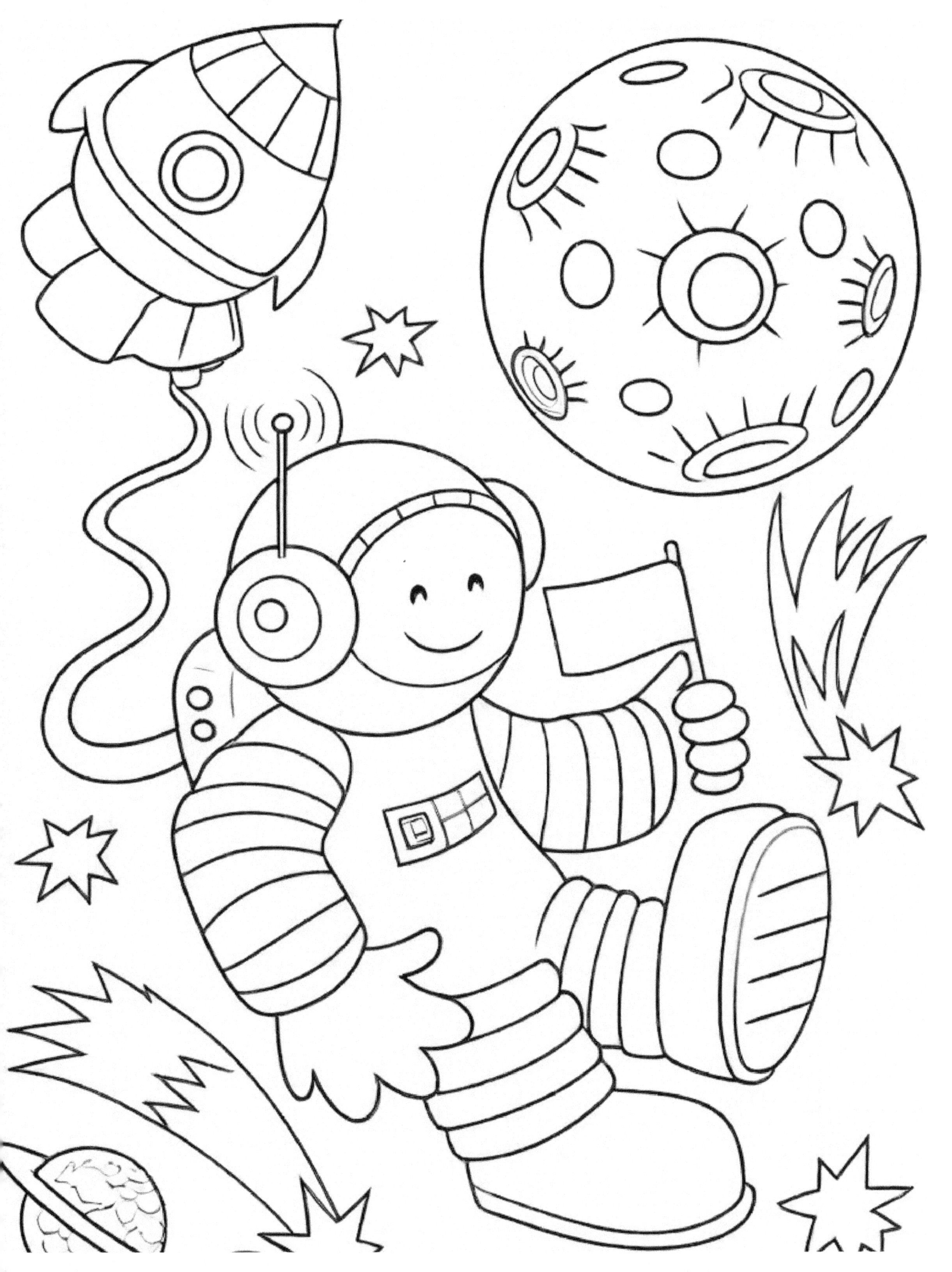

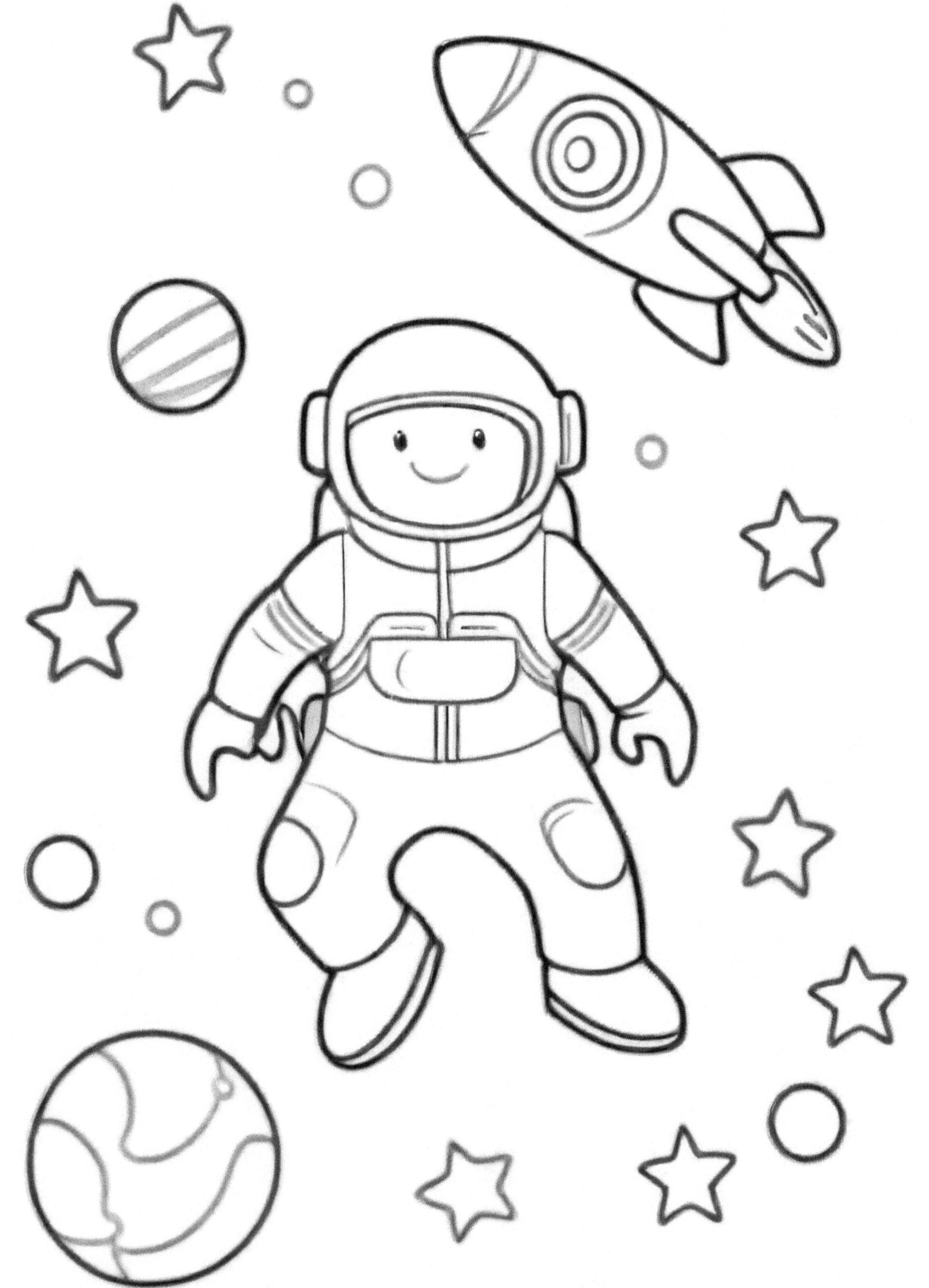

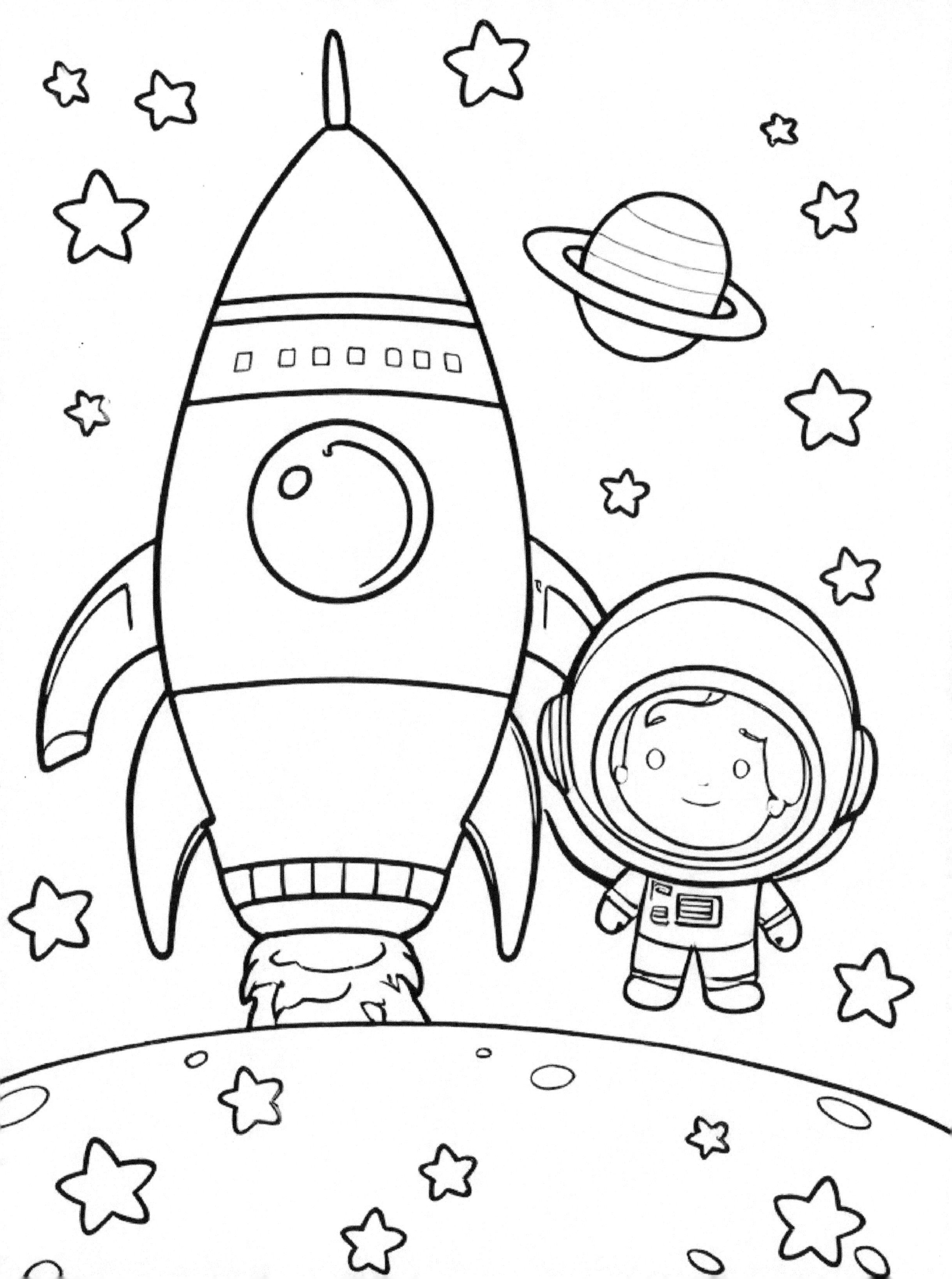

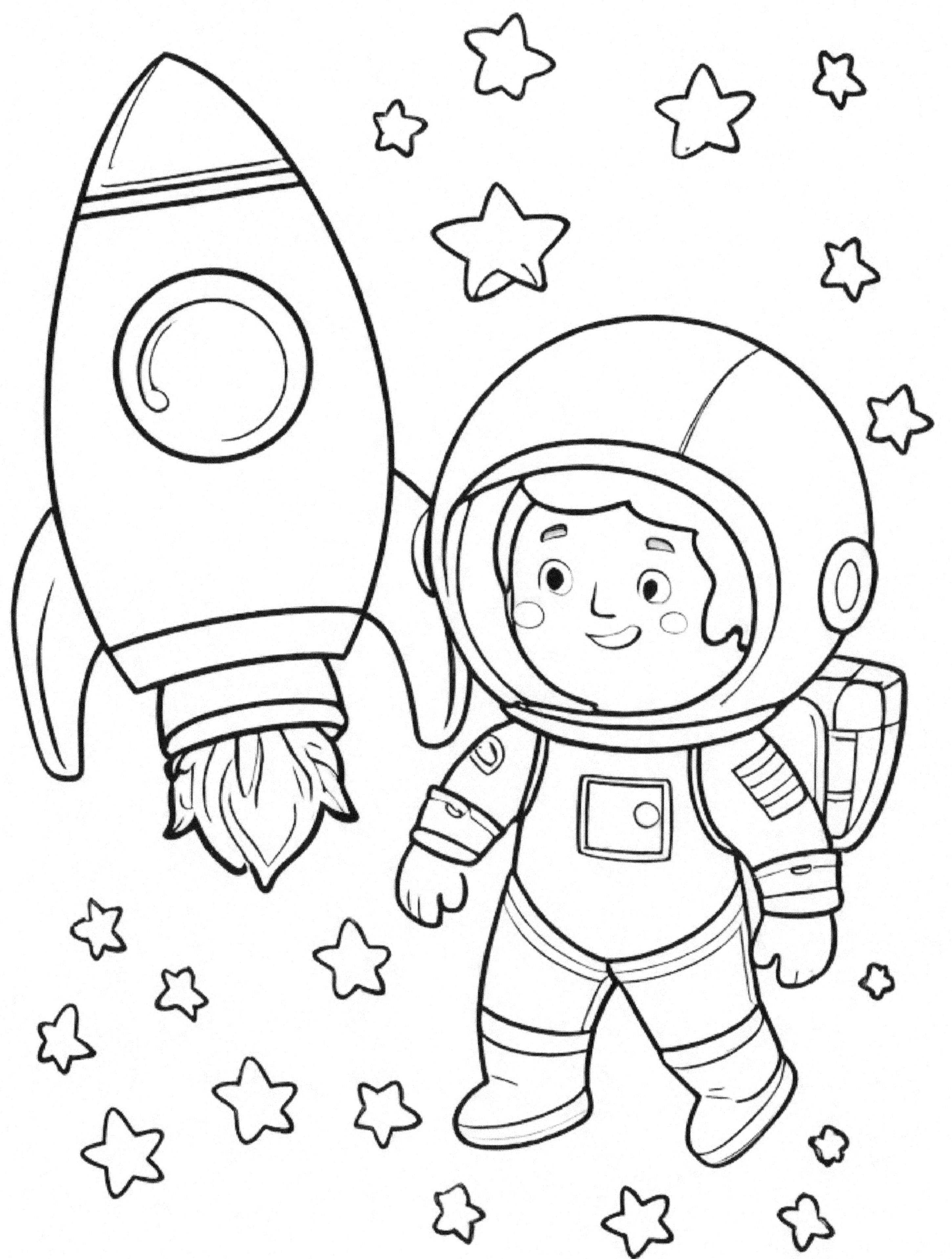

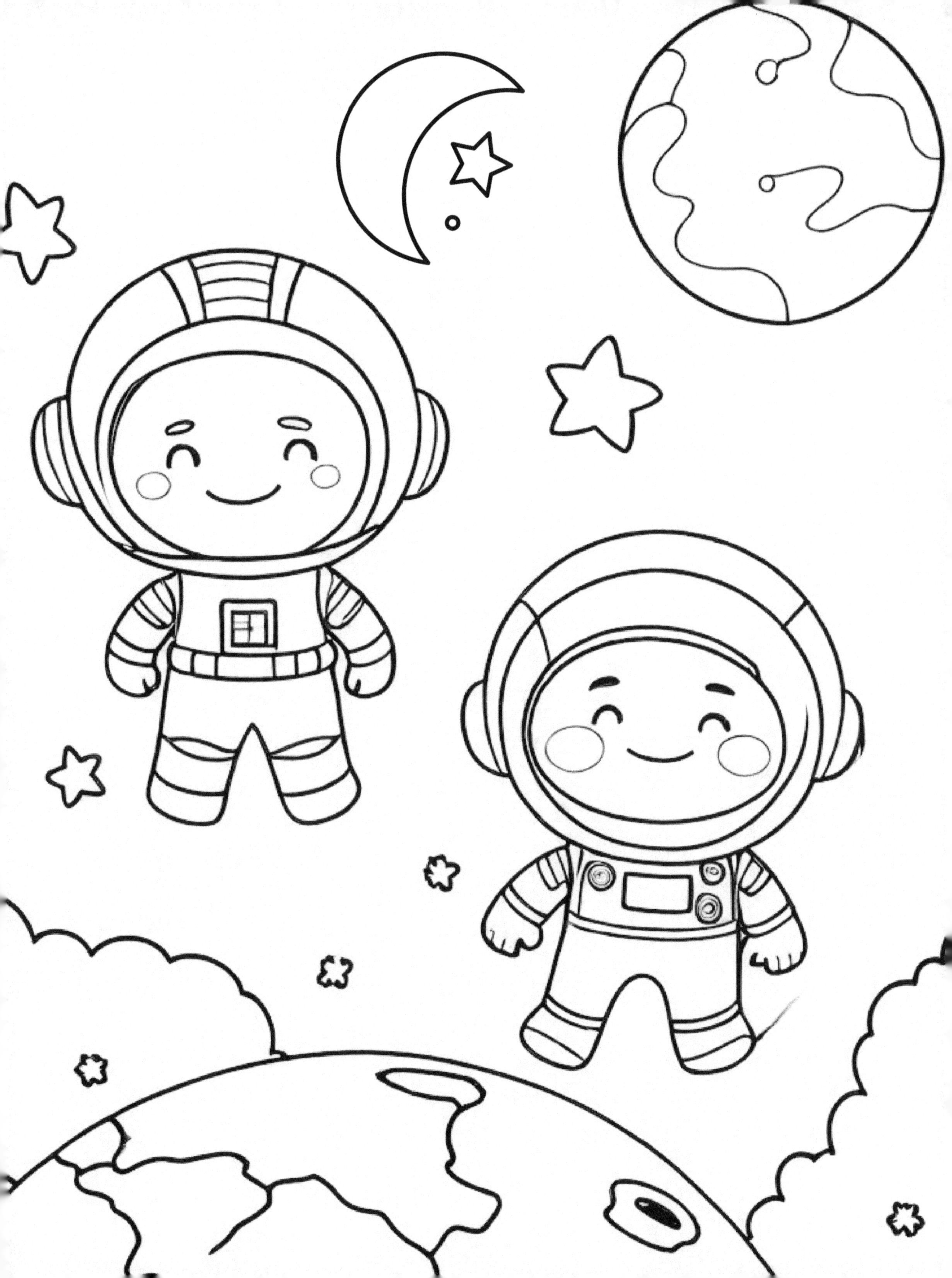